First edition copyright © 2023 Luna Charles. All rights reserved. No part of this publication may be reproduced, stored in a retrieval system, or transmitted in any form or by any means, electronic, mechanical, photocopying, recording, or otherwise, without the publisher's prior written permission.

Also, By Luna Charles

Men Are Not the Problem
- Vol I, II & III

My Life, My Rules
- Vol I & II

The Door – Short

The Healer's Persecution – Short

The Choices Made – Short

In the Beginning – Short
- Part of the Lilith Series

Good Food – BK 1 Vol I

Good Food - BK 1 Vol II

Good Food - BK 1 Vol III

As above, so below, as within, so without. – Hermetic quote

Chapter 1 – What and How

Human beings are a conscious representation of the macrocosm in a microform. Our evolution, reproduction, and manifestation cycles all work following Universal Laws. Plant, sow, and reap cycles did not speed up universally because the intelligence of our minds has invented technologies that sped up other areas of our lives. Divine intelligence does not understand microwaves and watches.

Like the world, we are made of the elements and create with the elements when in alignment. We must understand all elemental energies are slow but purposeful in their movements. Even fire, air, and water, which seem fast, took time to build up the force needed to move quickly. Think of the buildup to the explosion of a volcano, tsunami, or hurricane.

When we learn to control and work with our energy instead of fighting against ourselves and our environment. We learn how to manifest with spiritual energy by doing short-term hard work for long-term rewards. Rather than angrily manipulate energy for short-term gains and long-term karma.

FIRE – ACTION

WATER- EMOTIONS/SUBCONSCIOUS/FEMININE

AIR- LOGIC/CONSCIOUS/MASCULINE

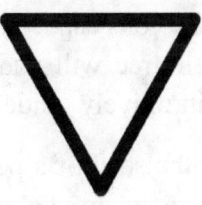

EARTH – DISCIPLINE

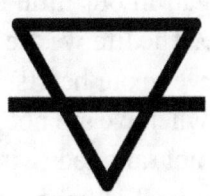

Media hype and false narratives have people believing that success is an overnight phenomenon. While hypocritically stating in the same sentence, the "overnight success" has been working on their craft all their lives. No one is an overnight success who has been working and perfecting their craft for decades.

That success story has been planting and sowing with God continuously. Despite all the opposition they faced. They fought wars against enemies we will never know to make enough ripples in the universe to cause a tipping point that could no longer be ignored. Which we superficially call an "overnight success" since knowledge of them only recently got to us.

However, on the macrocosm, they were on a path of destiny, on a timeline written for them, for what might have seemed like eons especially if it took them some time to get their free will and physical life in alignment with their intuitively guided, destined life.

We all carry the seed of a perfect timeline of the life we should live in our hearts. Implanted by Spirit, at the moment, our hearts first started beating. Before any other organ in our little bodies took form. Yet, most of the time. The life we are living is not what we feel like we deserve in our hearts. These differences in timelines happen when we are not in alignment with ourselves. We are not aligned with where we are supposed to be for several reasons.

One reason may be our fear of going down the path alone. Failing to understand our way, even with our partner, is always meant to be walked alone. Supported by each other, parallel to one another but still alone. Like a great Sequoia amongst a forest of Sequoias. Another reason might be that we are out of alignment due to trauma that must be healed, which also keeps us in fear.

Yet another reason may be others who see our true potential and purposely, through various means, keep us astray while manipulating us into dimming our light because they suffer from one or more cardinal sins. i.e., JEALOUSY, ENVY, GREED, WRATH, SLOTH, PRIDE and LUST.

The last part is what I hope this composition will help you with.

The truth is God is not responsible for our prosperity or protection. They gave us the power and the mind to control these things. They are only accountable for justice when things are beyond our control. Even then, we must ask for help.

Whether we choose to believe it or not, The Universe is a fair and balanced place. In all creation, the seed of what is planted will always eventually give a fruit of that seed. When our vision is narrow, we only focus on what we see. We will believe the universe is unfair. Millions are born in the most heinous of circumstances. At the same time, others are born into unbelievable wealth. Some must deal with the unfairness that society has created for them even before they are born. At the same time, others must live in the shadows of the name they are born into. Neither of these circumstances guarantees happiness. None are guaranteed to come with loving parents who nourish and protect them. None of them are guaranteed loyal friends and loved ones.

With all my heart, I suggest you not practice some things in this book if you haven't dived deep into your shadow work. The items will be specially marked (****). This is not a tool for revenge, spite, or frivolous pursuits. Because Divine Justice is just that, Just. Spirit's sword is twofold. Whatever you wish on someone will be visited on you. So, make sure your heart and actions are up to the scrutiny.

Also, before dismissing someone as not being of God because of their appearance, dress, or status, remember God has never picked Popes, Kings, or Princes to be prophets. There are sex workers who are more pious than preachers. Our definition of Godly is a social construct. One created to separate rather than unite. We need to understand the more we think we know God, with absolution. The further we move from divinity. To evolve, we need to put importance where it needs to be on the message, not the messenger.

There is a Hermetic saying that has proven repeatedly to be true throughout my life.

"When the student is ready, the teacher will appear."

But over the years, I have also learned the truth of this quote.

"When the student is ready, the teacher will disappear." – Tao Te Ching.

I've been blessed to be presented with various teachers throughout my journey—some on the material 3D plane and some on the 5D plane. Of course, in the beginning, when I was young, I didn't understand what lucid dreaming was, much less ethereal conscious beings. With age comes wisdom, at least for some of us. With age, I started to understand everything around me, including myself, is made of energy. Energy doesn't die because the physical body it inhabits deteriorates.

However, our Spirit is affected by what happens to our physical body. Especially the traumas that replay in minds and in the subconscious. These replays will slit us from our spiritual connection if we don't learn what happens to our matter/physical body manner to our Spirit. Our physical body reflects Spirit, and Spirit reflects back in the life you find yourself living. Since, in the grand scheme of things, Spirit is all that matters.

Therefore, one of our pillars of life should be to keep a positively charged physical body by keeping a positive mind healed from trauma and free of guilt as we approach each day with the knowledge of our connection to 'The All.' And with the noblest wishes for all, who wish no harm to us and others. Everyone else can deal with karma and divine justice. Remember, wrath is the lord's domain.

This is also why I believe there's absolutely no reason a stranger should be able to slide into your DM, email, or whatever electronic communication you have. And convince you that your ancestor reached out to them for them to give you a cleansing or reading or rebalancing to connect with the spiritual realm. Spirituality is very personal, as should be your relationship with God (your parents may have several children, but you don't vibe with your parents the same way as your siblings). Higher power allows and directs all other energies, including that of your ancestors.

Your ancestor will not reach out to somebody you've never met, never interacted with, and don't know from a can of paint to help you. Most messages are time-sensitive, so they will not risk expelling the energy to end up in your spam. If you reached out to that person first, then maybe.

But if that person has never met you in real life. You're not following them. You didn't brush against them while you were walking on the street. There has never been an energy interaction with them before they contacted you. It's a scam. Stay the f*** away from them.

You must start trusting and learning to read your energy to understand when your ancestors are trying to speak to you. Or a higher spiritual power is trying to connect to you. You're just not paying attention because it happens daily and around you. God never intended that our evolution should cost us financially. However, part of it is healing past trauma; counseling takes money. But your spiritual evolution should be free.

Chapter 2 – Prayers, Protection & Cord Cutting

Narcissism is nothing new. Back in the day, narcissists were called energy vampires. What is now called the narcissist's need to acquire residual benefits for survival? Then, were Vampires feeding off spiritual energy and everything that manifests from divine connections. Then, the groups that met to speak ill of others and project misfortune onto others were called covens. Now, have been modernized into flying monkeys.

Although psychology is just now understanding narcissism and its necessity for residual benefits. We in the spiritual community have always understood energy vampires and how they feed off other people to maintain themselves.

Whatever the term that we use for these people. Their existence and their tactics are not new. The only difference is now, we're relearning how to fight them. The same way our ancestors used to, without the fear imposed on us by people who wish to control our divine spiritual gift by fear.

These people, too, feed on our lack of wisdom. They feed when we fail to protect our family and ourselves. Since they are the ones we seek out for help when we face unknown, malicious spiritual attacks preventing us from truly reaching the peak of our personal evolutions.

We pray for the forgiveness of our enemies and daily bread. Then, we become upset when we falsely believe our prayers go unanswered. Yet if we paid close attention, we would notice that the enemies we're praying for continue to increase while our lives remain the same, but we do get our daily bread. That is because, with your words, you are using the positive karma that should have increased your daily bread to nullify the bad karma that that person should be receiving who has hurt.

And as long as you're telling the universe you deserve that treatment and are happy with your bread, that's all you'll get. Ask, and it is given.

If you will learn anything more from Jesus, I beg you to remember this. The people you pray for will serve you out to be sacrificed out of jealousy before your mission is done if you don't protect yourself from them.

Some people are easier to protect yourself from than others. In this first backfire book, we are going for easy and quick. Because I feel the need to get this out before the year's end. Things like learning to protect yourself and break energetic bonds with family and ex-spouses will take more than just candles in twine. You will also have to purge your life from the trauma they inflicted by speaking your truth. You will have to remove reminders of these people. Everything from clothing, pictures, and presents will have to go. Otherwise, you still have a cord from your past connected to the future. It's a cord that provides an open door and access to your spiritual being.

I will go through these kinds of purges in my videos, within pages of my books, and in future Backfire books.

It is not enough to speak our truth and move away from these people. We must cleanse our environment of items that hold a significant emotional weight.

We cannot think clearly and evolve fully until we feel at peace and safe. Although we cannot create harmony in all the places, we find ourselves. We can at least make it in our homestead and guard the peace there.

Finally, you will notice I don't say Amen at the end of my prayers. I stopped a while back after realizing that amen meant, so it be. It's like a command. I don't believe in commanding Spirit or the energy around us. We're supposed to work with them in vibration and in frequency.

Prayer 1 -

Holy Father (Divine Mother) Hollow be thy name. Thy kingdom comes, thy will and justice be done on Earth as in heaven. Thank you today and every day for my endless flow of abundance. The abundance of health, wealth, divine love, and protection for myself, my children, the people I love, and the innocent.

Thank you for the many gifts that you have imparted to me. The gifts that grow daily as my understanding and control of them grow each day. Thank you for guiding my steps, protecting me from my enemies, and giving me strength to persevere on the journey you have set before me. Thank you for your grace and unconditional love.

Prayer 2 -

Holy Father, Divine Mother, I add this home under your protective umbrella. May you bestow your protection, unconditional love, understanding, and strength to persevere to its inhabitants. May all negativity that tries to enter this home be returned to its master with loving detachment speedily by your divine protection.

Protecting yourself.

Depending on the situation, draw a physical circle around you and those in need using salt(sea) and red brick dust (ochre). Start Calling the name of your ancestors and your Lwa as you draw a circle of white fire around you and those close to you.

Repeat:

This is the moment.

This is the time.

This is the hour.

I invoke in myself.

All my ancestral power to protect myself.

Cutting cords –

Materials

1 white candle

twine cord

Brown paper

#2 pencil

Procedure

Write small to fit on brown paper with a number two pencil -

In the name of the most high God, the guardians assigned to me, the ancestors allowed to stand by my side, and the spirits here to guide me. Using my free will, I release myself from any and all bindings placed on me, unknowingly or knowingly, through trauma and coercion. Any and all bindings to my health, wealth, intuition, creativity, and clarity. From any and all sources, throughout time and space, from this point forward and back.

(Furthermore, I bind my energy to myself so that one may use it without my explicit permission or face instant karma for the attempt. ****)

Wrap the brown paper around the white candle. Tie them with the twine cord by wrapping it seven times around the candle. Finish at the bottom of the candle...

Place everything in a safe place so that the candle, cord, and brown paper can burn overnight. Thus, releasing the energy cords that bind you as the cord, the paper and candle burn.

Incantation for your doors

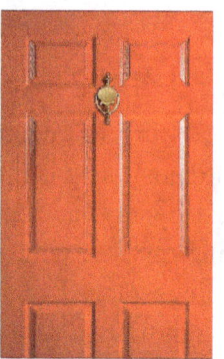

Energy returns three times three, as you feel and speak, so it shall be. will, action, knowledge

-passed through this threshold of positive thought and open heart. All you wish in mind and heart will return to you three times as fast and smart.

Shielding your homestead

Needed Materials -

- A gallon of seawater OR a hand full of sea salt
- 1 gallon of rainwater or any water that HAS NOT been through a pipe SYSTEM.
- 1 stick Palo Santo
- 1 white candle or 2 if there is more than one floor.
- A lighter
- clean white towels
- Bare feet

PROCEDURE -

This procedure is a TWO PERSON job. (This second person should be highly trusted and a positive person in your life. If they're going to be living there with you, even better.

IF USING SEA WATER SKIP to "OPENING OF WINDOWS AND DOORS."

Mix sea salt in water until salt is completely diluted.

Once you and your partner have opened all the windows and doors that lead to the outside of the house or condominium.

Light the white candle in the center of the house.

One person will portion the water from the gallon into a small, malleable container. Then, starting at the front door, move in a clockwise direction, pour a very thin line of water around the home's interior (through every bedroom, office, kitchen, and any room has a wall connecting to the outside world or the neighbors).

While the second person lights the Palo Santo and follows behind the first person, repeating prayer 2 (found in this composition).

You must imagine the seawater and the smoke entangling to become a white shield-like barrier around your homestead.

Once you reach the front door, repeat the prayer together. Think you're home for taking care of you as you will take care of it, with love and care.

Now, a clockwise position starting with the front door closes all your windows and doors. Let the water seep into the home for about an hour before wiping off any access residue and mopping it with white towels.

I suggest immediately doing something fun or funny in the home to seal the positive energy.

Return to sender with love - ****

I call upon the protective Spirit of the Divine Mother and Holy Father. I seek the hand of divine justice and Karmic balancing. I asked that those I do no pain, who speak my name in vain. Who seek an increase in personal wealth by marring my reputation and self-esteem to death. See Not a rise but slow demise in all they seek of enterprise. A lowering standard of luck for each time they use my name as muck. As I move forward in purpose. Leaving your wrath for whoever deserves it.

Chapter 3 - Fruits, Herbs and Spices

Everything around us is a manifestation of the Divine. Every expression serves several purposes for our benefit. It is part of our education here to learn to work with these different manifestations of God. For one, to better understand God in its many forms. And two, to help us move down our path as quickly and positively as possible.

When we learn to see God in everything, down to the everyday items we use and eat. We know a profound lesson about the saying, 'God is Love.' That we are part of a great cosmic spiritual family.

Allspice

Allspice refers to the dried berries of the plant Pimenta dioica. It was given that name because its flavor combines Cinnamon, nutmeg, cloves, pepper, juniper, and ginger. It has anti-inflammatory properties, aids digestion, boosts immunity, contains antioxidants, helps with dental health, and improves circulation.

In Spiritual Work –

Allspice is used in spells for money, luck, and healing. Burn-dried Allspice for these functions or carry the barriers in the satchel for the same purpose. In addition, Allspice is helpful in all healing mixtures.

Recipe suggestion -

Add Allspice to teas, soups, or sauces for its healing properties and personal luck daily.

Aloe

It has antioxidant and antibacterial properties to accelerate wound healing. It reduces dental plaque and treats canker sores. In addition, it relieves constipation and may improve skin and prevent wrinkles.

In Spiritual Work -

Lore states that growing an aloe plant in your house will help prevent household accidents, mainly burns. In Africa, aloe plants hang over doors to bring luck and destroy evil.

Recipe suggestion -

Add aloe to your everyday smoothies for a more robust immune system and better skin.

Apples

The apple contains phytochemicals and fiber, which carry antioxidants that may protect a cell's DNA from oxidative damage, a precursor to cancer. Apples improve gut health and reduce the risk of stroke, high blood pressure, and diabetes. They are a good source of vitamin C and low in Sodium, fat, and cholesterol.

In Spiritual Work -

On Halloween night, see a vision of your future partner. With the light out, light a candle and cut an apple into nine pieces. Eat eight while gazing in the mirror. Pierce the ninth piece with your knife and hold it over your shoulder. The apparition of your future partner is said to appear and take it.

Recipe suggestion -

Bake thin apple slices for a healthy, anytime snack.

Apricots

Apricots are rich in potassium, phosphorus, and beta-carotene, which the body converts to vitamin A and other carotenoids. Apricots are excellent for promoting eye health. They contain Lutein, which helps to support retina and lens health.

In Spiritual Work -

The leaves and flowers can be added to love sachets, and the pits are carried to attract love.

Recipe suggestion –

Add sun-dried Apricots to salads. Or eat the day as an everyday snack.

Bay Leaf

Bay leaf is a good source of vitamin A, vitamin B6, and vitamin C. These vitamins are all known to support a healthy immune system. Bay leaf tea can help ease bouts of upset stomachs. It can help relieve sinus pressure or a stuffy nose. Reduces type 2 diabetes risk factors.

In Spiritual Work -

Use the Bay leaves to write down things you wish to manifest or release and then burn them in ritual. Keep bay leaves on your person when performing any healing rituals or when you're about to do something that you want to succeed at.

Recipe suggestion –

Add to soup, sauces, or teas to benefit from immune-boosting properties.

Black Pepper

Loaded with potassium, magnesium, iron, vitamin K, and vitamin C, black pepper is a vital healing spice in Ayurveda Medicine. Black pepper helps to fight against infections and insect bites. In addition, it helps fight tooth decay and provides quick relief from toothache.

In Spiritual Work -

Banish negativity, protect from an enemy, and keep unwanted people away by mixing black, salt, red, and Sulphur. Place the mixture in a container and hide it under the enemy's doorstep or where it must be walked over.

Recipe suggestion –

Add black pepper to anything, even margaritas.

Bluebells

The Bluebells are a flower that looks exactly like its name suggests. It is used as a remedy for leucorrhea and as a diuretic or styptic. Also, part of the stalk is used to make glue.

In Spiritual Work –

Add Bluebells to a garden to attract butterflies, bees, birds, or fairies. Or wear Bluebells as a hair ornament or a lei to compel someone to tell you the truth.

Recipe suggestion –

Do not eat. Poisonous

Calamus Root

Calamus root is known to be poisonous. However, despite safety concerns, it is still used to make medicine. For example, it is commonly used to cure stomach problems, including ulcers, inflammation of the stomach lining (gastritis), diarrhea, intestinal gas (flatulence), upset stomach, and many more.

In Spiritual Work –

The Calamus root is an aphrodisiac. It promotes harmony, love, and peace. It also strengthens binding spells. Burn some calamus incense before a job interview or meeting to encourage self-confidence and success.

Recipe suggestion -

Use Calamus root in tea to help with digestion problems.

Cardamom

Cardamom is rich in powerful phytonutrients and is exceptionally high in manganese, a trace mineral that helps the body form connective tissue, bones, and sex hormones. As a result, cardamom is the natural treatment for cancer, diabetes, bad breath, high blood pressure, and digestion problems.

In Spiritual Work –

The queen of spice is also the queen of love and lust. Chew cardamom seeds before speaking to a would-be lover or before an audience to keep their attention.

Recipe suggestion -

Add Cardamon to porridges and puddings.

Chestnuts

Chestnuts remain a good source of antioxidants, even after cooking. They're rich in gallic acid and ellagic acid—two antioxidants that increase in concentration when cooked. Antioxidants and minerals like magnesium and potassium help reduce your risk of cardiovascular issues, such as heart disease or stroke.

In Spiritual Work –

Chestnuts can be eaten to encourage fertility and desire and may be carried as a charm by women who wish to conceive. Keeping Chestnuts around the house (and eating them) encourages abundance.

Recipe suggestion –

Roast Chestnut for a healthy side dish (add some black pepper).

Chili Pepper

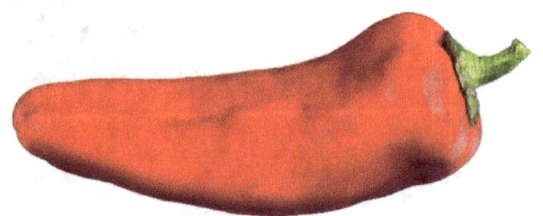

Red hot chili pepper fights inflammation and cardiovascular disease. In addition, it is a natural pain reliever, clears congestion, and boosts immunity. It is also known to help stop the spread of prostate cancer, prevent stomach ulcers, support weight loss, and lower the risk of Type 2 diabetes.

In Spiritual Work -

Fidelity, love, and hex breaking. Add chili pepper to a love spell to spice things up in the relationship.

Recipe suggestion -

Mix Garlic, Chili pepper, and lime for a delicious hot pepper sauce.

Cinnamon

One of the most beneficial spices on Earth, Cinnamon, has antioxidant, anti-inflammatory, anti-diabetic, antimicrobial, immunity-boosting, potential cancer, and heart disease-protecting abilities. In addition, it helps defend the brain against developing neurological disorders such as Parkinson's and Alzheimer's.

In Spiritual Work -

It is used to gain wealth and success. Before a big meeting, mix a dash of Cinnamon into hand lotion. Moisturize your hands while visualizing a successful outcome in your favor. Shake every decision-maker's hand that is present.

Recipe suggestion –

Try adding Cinnamon to your coffee or tea.

Cleavers

Cleavers enhance the lymphatic system's function and improve its ability to flush out toxins, decrease congestion, and reduce swelling. The lymph-cleansing action of this herb, in turn, enhances the immune system's function.

In Spiritual Work –

Cleavers are commonly used in binding spells and matters of commitment. Use bits or mojo bags that deal with commitment issues, rocky relationships, and love.

Recipe suggestion -

Chop and boil Cleavers to make a blood-cleansing tea.

Comfrey

Comfrey is also known as Boneset, Black roots, Black wort, Bruisewort, or Knit bone. Comfrey is a tea for upset stomachs, ulcers, heavy menstrual periods, diarrhea, bloody urine, persistent cough, painful breathing, bronchitis, cancer, and chest pains.

In Spiritual Work -

Comfrey is used magically for health, healing, protection during travel and prosperity. Keep a satchel with Comfrey on your person when traveling to keep you safe, or place some in your luggage to protect it from being stolen.

Recipe suggestion –

Use dry Comfrey, olive, and coconut oil to salve for pain.

Coriander

Coriander herb acts as a diuretic, which can help flush extra Sodium from your system and reduce your blood pressure. In addition, research suggests that coriander can help lower "bad" LDL cholesterol, reducing your risk of atherosclerosis, a form of coronary heart disease.

In Spiritual Work -

Coriander and its seeds are used for love, lust, and sex magic. Coriander helps to arouse your partner's desire, have sex last longer, and aids in fertility in women. Coriander also aids in divination and spirit communication. It Increases mental clarity and strengthens your third eye awareness.

Recipe suggestion –

Add coriander to any meat recipes for extra flavor.

Damiana Leaf

Damiana, or Feuille de Damiana, is an herb commonly found in Mexico. It is widely used by mouth as an aphrodisiac to treat sexual problems. It also treats stomach issues such as dyspepsia, diarrhea, and constipation, improving menopause and premenstrual syndrome symptoms.

In Spiritual Work –

Damiana is called the herb of love for its aphrodisiac properties. Used in love spells to attract new love or to return a straying lover. (WE DO NOT RECOMMEND LOVE SPELLS IN ANY WAY).

Recipe suggestion –

Drink a tea made of Damiana leaf to heighten sexual desire on date night.

Dates

Dates are a superfruit delivering various benefits to the brain, digestive system, and heart. Dates are particularly rich in vitamins A, B6, and K. Those vitamins promote bone growth and improve eye health. In addition, dates contain anti-cancer agents, help during childbirth, and fibers reduce belly fat. They also prevent hair loss and promote healthy hair.

In Spiritual Work –

Dates and dried pieces of palm can be worn to harness fertility energy.

Recipe suggestion –

Stuff Dates with goat cheese and sprinkle with honey for a girl's night, pre-party.

Devil's Claw

Devil's Claw, or Harpagophytum procumbens, is a traditional medicinal plant of the San people of the Kalahari Desert. Devil's Claw is a perennial desert plant, recognizable by its purple flowers, fruits, and voluminous roots. It treats diseases and relieves joint pains, muscle aches, and digestive disorders. It also treats urinary tract infections, ulcers, and blood diseases.

In Spiritual Work –

Strong protective magic. Carry in a mojo bag for protection. Hang it over the home's entry doors to prevent evil from entering. Use Sage or Santo Palo to cleanse by burning.

Recipe suggestion –

I have none. If you have one, DM me @Mslunacharles

Dragon's Blood

Dragon's Blood has a proven healing effect on wounds, is antimicrobial, and forms a protective layer over the skin, helping keep germs away. It is anti-inflammatory and pro-collagen, making it a sought-after skincare ingredient. It is also known as an antioxidant thanks to its natural flavonoids.

In Spiritual Work –

Dragon's Blood has been used as a ritual to neutralize negative energy. A pinch of dragon's Blood increases the potency and effectiveness of other herbs in an incense mixture. Also, use it for money-drawing or love-drawing spells.

Recipe suggestion –

I have none. If you have one, DM me @Mslunacharles

Elderberry

Elderberry is a dark purple berry from the European elder tree. Elderberry prevents and fights the common cold, influenza, and H1N1 "swine" flu. It is also taken by mouth for HIV/AIDS and boosts the immune system. Elderberry can also help with sinus pain, back and leg pain (sciatica), nerve pain (neuralgia), and chronic fatigue syndrome.

In Spiritual Work –

The Elderberry can be used for good and evil. Grow close to the home to protect it from evil beings. Or use elder water to bless items before a ritual.

Recipe suggestion –

Elderberry tea

Fennel

Fennel is a flowering plant species in the carrot family. It is a hardy, perennial herb with yellow flowers and feathery leaves indigenous to the Mediterranean's shores. Fennel seeds have antioxidant, anti-inflammatory, antifungal, and antiviral effects.

In Spiritual Work –

To use for all-around defense, plant fennel around your house. Fennel seeds can be placed close to windows to ward off evil spirits and unwelcome guests.

Recipe suggestion –

Add Fennel seeds to your dry rub for ribs.

Figs

Figs improve digestion, decrease constipation, and help manage blood fat and sugar. Figs contain calcium, copper, magnesium, potassium, phosphorus, iron, and vitamins A, B6, C, and K.

In Spiritual Work -

Eat the fruit of this tree to make it easier to connect to divine knowledge and your Higher Self.

Recipe suggestion –

Add to your fruit smoothie.

Garlic

Garlic has excellent health-promoting and disease-preventing effects on many common human diseases, such as cancer, cardiovascular and metabolic disorders, blood pressure, and diabetes, through its antioxidant, anti-inflammatory, and lipid-lowering properties.

In Spiritual Work -

Garlic can be used in banishing. Hang a braid of twelve heads of garlic over your door to banish jealous people and thieves.

Recipe suggestion –

Add that ish to everything!

Ginger

Ginger is known to help digestion, reduce nausea (which is excellent when you're pregnant or for a hangover), and help combat the flu and the common cold. In addition, as a potent anti-inflammatory and antioxidant, ginger can combat seasickness, reduce muscle pain, drastically lower blood sugars, improve heart disease risk factors, and significantly reduce menstrual pain.

In Spiritual Work –

Love, money, power, and success. Plant a ginger root in your house to attract wealth.

Recipe suggestion –

Drink Ginger tea for hangovers.

Ginseng

Ginseng is commonly touted for its antioxidant and anti-inflammatory effects. It could also help regulate blood sugar levels and benefit certain types of cancer. Ginseng also strengthens the immune system, enhances brain function, reduces fatigue, and improves symptoms of erectile dysfunction.

In Spiritual Work –

Ginseng is a "Wonder of the World Root" that will grant a wish etched onto a root placed under running water. To make a Success Satchel, place Ginseng Root, Black Cohosh, Red Clover, and John the Conqueror Root with Iron Pyrite in a bag.

Recipe suggestion –

Add Ginseng to your smoothie for an immune booster.

Grapes

Grapes contain antioxidants, vitamin C, potassium, and vitamin K. They may help prevent type 2 diabetes and lower blood pressure. In addition, the nutrients in grapes may help protect against cancer, eye problems, and cardiovascular disease.

In Spiritual Work –

Plant a vine near your magical garden as a form of garden magic to attract abundance into your space and life.

Recipe suggestion –

Eat Grapes.

Hemp

Hemp seeds and foods rich in Gamma-Linolenic acid (GLA) like hemp seeds have also been observed to help people with ADHD, breast pain, diabetes, diabetic neuropathy, heart disease, high blood pressure, multiple sclerosis, obesity, premenstrual syndrome, rheumatoid arthritis, skin allergies.

In Spiritual Work –

Hemp can intensify a vision quest when burned like incense while meditating. It shares the same energy as clear quartz and is a natural amplifier.

Recipe suggestion –

Add Hemp seeds to your ice cream.

Honey

Raw honey contains chemicals that act as antioxidants and antidepressants. It may also help with convulsions and anxiety. Honey is used in Ayurvedic medicine for treating imbalances in the body. In Ancient Egyptian, it was used to treat wounds, sweeten cakes and biscuits, and embalm the dead.

In Spiritual Work –

Honey sweetens someone's feelings towards you. In one traditional spell, love is poured into a jar or saucer on top of a slip of paper containing the person's name.

Recipe suggestion –

Replace sugar with honey.

Horsetail

Horsetail weed or Equisetum arvense is a general antioxidant and is considered a super herb by some. Horsetail has been used for traditional remedies for urinary tract infections, healing bones, strengthening hair and teeth, and keeping the skin wrinkle-free. It also helps with arthritis (rheumatoid and osteo), osteoporosis, weak bladder, and chronic lung disease.

In Spiritual Work –

Horsetail is an herb of strength. Grow horsetail on your property to reinforce a boundary spell or add it to an enchantment to reaffirm commitment in a relationship. It can also be used for snake charming (not recommended) and fertility.

Recipe suggestion –

I have none. If you have one, DM me @Mslunacharles

Juniper Berries

Like most other berries, they're a good source of vitamin C. Vitamin C is essential for immune health, collagen synthesis, and blood vessel function. It also acts as a potent antioxidant, protecting your cells from damage caused by unstable molecules called free radicals.

In Spiritual Work –

Cleanse with juniper water by placing the object dipped in an infusion of juniper needles and left in transparent glass on the windowsill overnight so that moonlight falls on the glass. To protect the house from people with impure thoughts and from evil spirits, juniper twigs are hung on the front door.

Recipe suggestion –

Garlic potatoes with Juniper berries.

Lavender

Lavender reduces anxiety and emotional stress. Protects against diabetes symptoms, improves brain function, helps heal burns and wounds, improves sleep, restores skin complexion, reduces acne, and slows the aging process with powerful antioxidants. Relieves pain. Alleviates headaches.

In Spiritual Work –

Love and chastity protection (when used with rosemary). Promotes purification, peace, longevity, and happiness. Place a small satchel of dried lavender under your pillow at night to help you sleep better.

Recipe suggestion –

Lavender tea

Licorice Root

Licorice root is known to aid heartburn and acid reflux, leaky gut, and adrenal fatigue. In addition, it is one of the main adaptogen herbs to lower cortisol. As a result, it helps immunity, coughs, sore throats, PMS, and menopause. It also relieves pain, regulates sebum production, and hydrates the skin.

In Spiritual Work –

Licorice is a root of love, fidelity, and commitment. Add licorice to a satchel with other commanding herbs and someone's name you wish to control. Drop the bag in the yard of their place of residence.

Recipe suggestion –

Caramelized carrots with licorice roots and ginger.

Lotus Root

Lotus root improves digestion, reduces cholesterol, lowers blood pressure, and boosts the immune system. In addition, it aids in preventing various forms of cancer. Furthermore, lotus root is rich in Vitamin C and has many medicinal benefits.

In Spiritual Work –

Burn Lotus root-like incense to bring inner peace and outer harmony to aid meditation and open the mind's eye.

Recipe suggestion –

Add Lotus root to your vegetable stir fry.

Mallow

Mallow is a plant that grows wild throughout North America. People use flowers and leaves to make medicine. Mallow is used for irritation of the mouth and throat, a dry cough, and bronchitis. It is also used for stomach and bladder problems.

In Spiritual Work –

Mallow is considered a reliable tool for attracting benevolent Spirits and grounding them in our realm for better communication. Smoke dry leaves on your altar when seeking aid.

Recipe suggestion –

Use to make flavored Marshmallows.

Milk Thistle

Milk thistle contains compounds that may support skin, liver, and bone health and enhance weight loss. Milk thistle might also help prevent insulin resistance and slow cancer growth, among other benefits.

In Spiritual Work –

Carry this herb with you, or leave it in a bowl. It will renew vitality. It is a protective amulet in mojo bags alongside other anti-hexing and cleansing herbs.

Recipe suggestion –

Milk thistle tea for a healthy liver.

Mint

Mint is an excellent source of vitamin A, a fat-soluble vitamin critical for eye health and night vision. It is also a potent source of antioxidants, especially compared to other herbs and spices. The antioxidants in mint help protect your body from oxidative stress, a type of damage to cells caused by free radicals.

In Spiritual Work –

Drinking mint tea can bring you good luck and protection throughout the day. Sometimes, the herb will be placed under a pillow to induce a vision of the future in dreams and to protect against attacks of evil magic, nightmares, and evil spirits of the night.

Recipe suggestion –

Switch up your pesto with mint.

Mugwort

Mugwort has historically been used as an herbal inhibitor for women's menstrual cycles and helps provide menopause relief. It's also used to reverse breech birth position, soothe and treat joint pain, and attack cancerous cells and malaria.

In Spiritual Work –

Mugwort is a visionary herb and induces psychic dreams and prophetic visions. Mugwort can be absorbed trans-dermally through lotions and can also be smoked.

Recipe suggestion –

Try Asian Mugwort soup.

Nutmeg

Nutmeg enhances heart and brain health, decreases inflammation, and treats insomnia. It also helps supply a small amount of several essential nutrients, including fiber, magnesium, calcium, and iron.

In Spiritual Work –

A whole nutmeg seed can be carried on your person to bring luck during games of chance (Bingo, cards, Dominoes). Add nutmeg to a beverage before meditation or divination to enhance clairvoyance, clear your sight, and encourage visions.

Recipe suggestion –

Nutmeg can be added to everything from cake to chicken.

Olives

Olives contain many vitamins and antioxidants. It helps against osteoporosis. It contains the compound oleocanthal, which studies have shown can kill cancer cells. The oleocanthal in olives and olive oil is linked to reduced risk for Alzheimer's disease and increases the activity of the drug donepezil, which is used to treat dementia.

In Spiritual Work –

Draw a pentagram in olive oil on an item you want to protect or wear olive leaves to bring good luck.

Recipe suggestion -

Try marinated olive salad.

Oregano

Oregano is a delicious herb found in most kitchen cabinets. It is rich in antioxidants and potent antibacterial, antifungal, and antiviral. It also helps fight cancer and decreases inflammation.

In Spiritual Work –

Oregano is feminine in energy. It is ruled by Venus and is considered an air element. Oregano can be used in spells involving luck, love, and happiness. Sleep with Oregano on your head for revealing dreams.

Recipe suggestion –

Lemon – oregano roasted vegetables.

Paprika

Paprika imparts a wide variety of health benefits, ranging from the treatment of rheumatoid arthritis and osteoarthritis to anemia prevention and even fuller, softer, healthier hair.

In Spiritual Works –

Boosting spell work, adding energy, fidelity, hex breaking, and love.

Recipe suggestion –

Make seafood rice with smoked paprika.

Pomegranate

Pomegranates contain potent anti-inflammatory, antioxidant, anti-obesity, and antitumor properties. The arils of the fruit are eaten fresh, and the juice is made into grenadine syrup. It is also used in flavorings and liqueurs. In addition, Pomegranate is high in dietary fiber, folic acid, vitamin C, and vitamin K.

In Spiritual Work –

Pomegranate seeds can be eaten to increase fertility, or the dried skin can be carried for the same purpose. The Pomegranate is a fruit shrouded in mystery and loved by many. This fruit is excellent for fertility, luck, and money-drawing spells. Use dried pomegranate skin in your incense bowl to invite money into your home.

Recipe suggestion –

Eat a pomegranate before wishing to help it come true.

Purple Corn

Purple Corn tends to reduce blood clots, fight against hypertension, and lower blood pressure. Promotes the creation of collagen and cell renewal as well as that of connective tissues. The Anthocyanins in purple Corn also help regulate and reduce cholesterol, improve blood circulation, eliminate toxins, and have an anti-inflammatory effect.

In Spiritual Work –

Purple Corn can be used in protection, luck, and divination spells. It's particularly effective when used to protect children. Simply place an ear of Corn in the bed your child sleeps in. Corn is a sign of a bountiful harvest and can also be used to encourage financial prosperity.

Recipe suggestion –

Chicha Morada

Rose

Roses can be used as a flower remedy and essential oil in tinctures, glycerites, teas, honey, oxymels, syrups, vinegar, and hydrosols. It's nutrient-rich, astringent, diuretic, and anti-inflammatory and also used for uplifting the spirits, grief, PMS, upset tummy, sore throats, colds, and during menopause.

In Spiritual Work –

Make a rose tea to boost sexuality and as an anti-inflammatory. Use candles to attract love. Burn rose petals and use the ashes to cut ties with a former lover. Add to a sachet for sleep to promote sweet dreams.

Recipe suggestion –

Rose Frosé.

Rosemary

Rosemary is known to improve memory, soothe digestive problems, boost the immune system, and relieve aches and pains. In addition, it discourages hair loss, promotes growth, cleans and strengthens the liver, lowers cortisol, and fights cancer.

In Spiritual Work –

After cleansing, bake a dish with rosemary when moving into a new place. The rosemary will help the house retain this new vibration as its own. When in need, burn it again so the scent will bring back memories and vibrations.

Recipe suggestion –

Rosemary roasted chicken.

Sage

Sage or salvia is a prevalent herb found in millions of kitchens. As a tea, it will help settle a sour stomach and ease digestion. In addition, it's rich in antioxidants, great for oral health, alleviates menopause symptoms, helps fight diabetes, and helps with memory loss.

In Spiritual Work –

Sage is used as a magical herb for protection and purification. But sage can be used in magical workings for immortality, longevity, wisdom, and granting wishes.

Recipe suggestion –

Cheese and sage stuffed chicken.

Salt

Salt or Sodium facilitates signals to our nerves and muscles. It also helps sustain the fluid content inside and outside the blood cells. As a result, it promotes good vascular health, balances electrolytes, prevents muscle cramping, and supports the nervous system.

In Spiritual Work –

A ritual bath with salt in the water or salt applied directly to the skin, often mixed with oil and then washed away, can help an individual rid him or herself of negative energy.

Recipe suggestion –

It's salt. Lol.

Spanish Needle

Spanish needles or Bidens Alba, as they are scientifically known. Are natural antibiotics. Powerfully anti-inflammatory, strongly antibacterial, fights urinary tract infections, and helps with chronic diarrhea, dysentery, gastritis, and ulcers. Assists in treating inflamed mucous membranes in colds and flu and respiratory infections of any sort, sore throats from coughs, disease or overuse of the throat, and vaginal infections.

In Spiritual Work –

Spanish Needle's magical properties include healing, purification, and fertility. Dip a bouquet of Spanish Needles into cold water and use the flowers to spread the water over an area you wish to cleanse.

Recipe suggestion –

Spanish needle tea.

Spikenard

Spikenard affects the three major nerve plexuses – cardiac, solar, and sacral. Spikenard can relax the brain and cardiovascular system, acting as a "strong hypnotic cerebral sedative" and a cardiovascular relaxant.

In Spiritual Work –

Spikenard is a classic anointing oil. It offers protection and purification for ritual work. It benefits spirit journeys to the Otherworld and may help those embarking on this last rite of passage.

Recipe suggestion –

Spikenard syrup.

Sorrel

Sorrel is exceptionally high in vitamin C, a water-soluble vitamin that fights inflammation and plays a crucial role in immune function. It's also high in fiber, promoting regularity, increasing feelings of fullness, and helping stabilize blood sugar levels.

In Spiritual Work –

Carry Sorrel to protect against heart disease. Place in sickrooms to aid in recuperation from illnesses and wounds.

Recipe suggestion –

Sorrel Juice.

Star Fruit

Starfruit is fiber-rich, containing around 60% cellulose, 27% hemicellulose, and 13% pectin. Starfruit includes many vitamins and minerals, including natural antioxidants such as vitamin C and gallic acid, which help prevent cellular damage.

In Spiritual Work –

Star fruit is believed to bring good luck and ward off evil. According to the principles of Feng Shui, the five-pointed stars on the skin of a star fruit represent wealth and happiness. In some cultures, Starfruits are placed near windowsills to encourage positive energy in the home.

Recipe suggestion –

Eat Star fruit like an apple.

Vervain

Vervain is a popular remedy due to its multiple plant-beneficial compounds. Some of its benefits include antitumor effects, nerve cell protection, anxiety- and convulsion-reducing properties, and antimicrobial activity.

In Spiritual Work –

Vervain has both purification ability and protective properties. It is used for cleansing and consecrating a sacred ritual space. It is also a protective herb. For example, Roman soldiers would carry vervain into battle, and people would sprinkle their homes with vervain to keep away evil Spirits.

Recipe suggestion –

Vervain tincture.

Wolfsbane

Poisonous Wolfbane is acclaimed in traditional herbal medicine due to its healing actions, which were considered analgesic, anti-rheumatic, sedative, fever-reducing, and anti-inflammatory. Wolfsbane is included in the treatment of joint and muscle pain. Also claimed that applying it to the skin slows the heart rate in cardiac patients.

In Spiritual Work –

Wolfbane is cited as a protective plant. It's beneficial for invoking Hecate, The Goddess of the Moon. It could be used in sympathetic magic to harm another by creating "elf bolts" of sharpened flint dipped in wolfsbane juice and piercing a poppet for the victim with them.

Recipe suggestion –

Nope. Poisonous.

Wormwood

Wormwood is an herb that can be used in supplement form. Potential benefits include symptom relief for Crohn's disease, aid with digestion, and lower arthritis pain. It also has antioxidant benefits.

In Spiritual Work –

Wormwood is a powerful apotropaic herb, which means that it protects from evil. Legend holds that Wormwood planted around your garden will keep pests and snakes away. It can be used for boundary magic and is burned in incense designed to aid in developing psychic powers and can also be worn for this reason. Carry it with you to protect you from bewitchment.

Recipe suggestion –

Add to tea.

About the author

Luna Charles, is a Haitian-American writer who has authored numerous books, articles, and essays. Besides being an accomplished author, Luna is also a dedicated student of Theology, Metaphysics, and Philosophy. As a mother of two lovely girls, Luna has spent most of her life in South Florida.

www.ingramcontent.com/pod-product-compliance
Lightning Source LLC
Chambersburg PA
CBHW072105290426
44110CB00014B/1833